Furry Logic

For Mark, Clare and Jamie.

Jane Seabrook

Furry Logic

A GUIDE TO LIFE'S LITTLE CHALLENGES

TEN SPEED PRESS
Berkeley

Smile

first thing

in the morning.

Get it over with.

I would be unstoppable.

If I could just get started.

Be yourself.

Nobody

is

better

qualified.

Life is

full of challenge

and frustration.

But sooner or later

you'll find the

hairstyle you like.

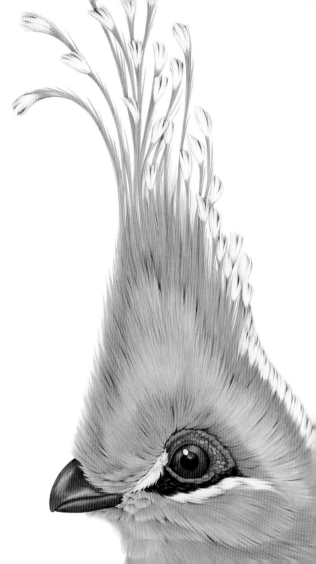

Always remember you are unique...

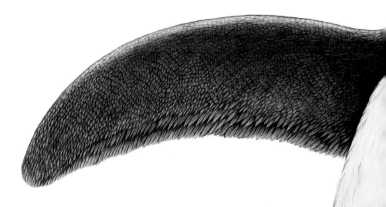

just like everyone else.

If at first

you do succeed,

try not to look

too astonished.

If at first

you don't succeed,

swallow all evidence

that you tried.

No one is listening

until you make a mistake.

I never made

Who's Who

but I'm featured in

What's That.

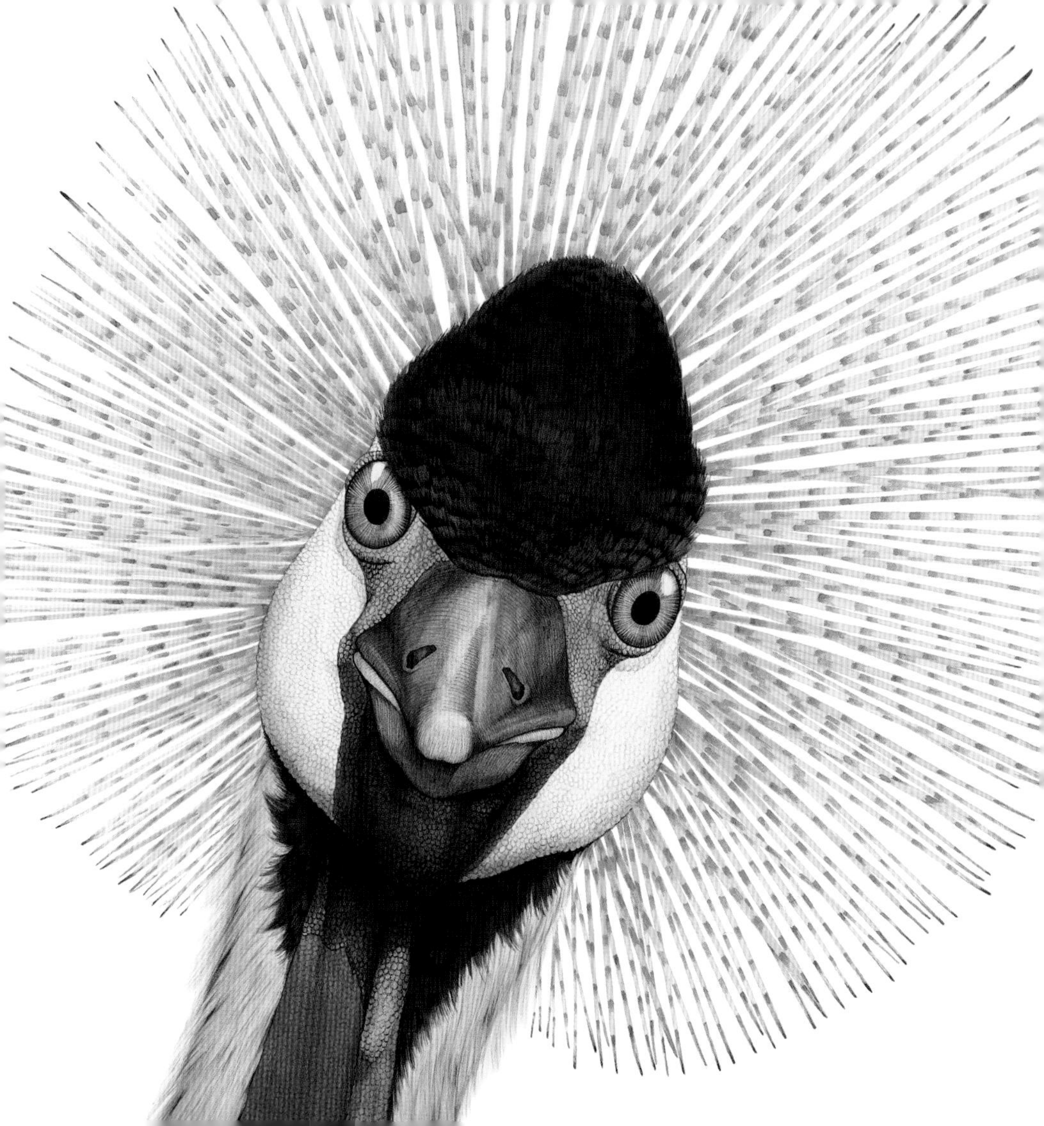

All power corrupts.

Absolute power is kinda neat.

The

trouble

with work

is ...

it's

so

daily.

I try to take

one day at a time ...

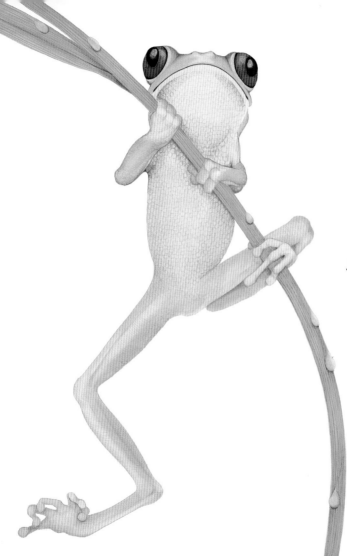

but

sometimes

several days

attack me

at once.

*I am **not** tense.*

Just terribly, terribly alert.

When you're in it up to your ears...

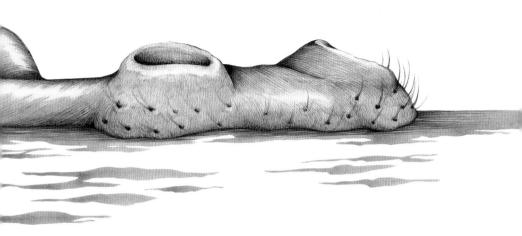

it pays to keep your mouth shut.

If

you can keep

your head when

all about you

are losing theirs -

It's quite possible

you haven't grasped

the situation.

I have one nerve left

and you're getting on it.

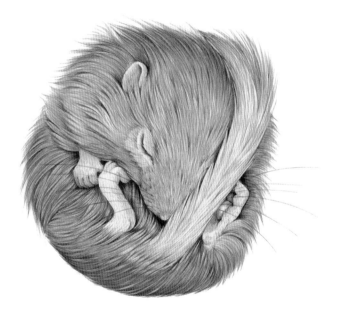

No day is so bad

that it can't be fixed

with a nap.

If you don't agree with me,

it means ...

you haven't been listening.

You don't have to agree

with me, but it's quicker.

Never go to bed mad -

stay up and fight.

You'll always be my best friend...

you

know

too

much.

Your secrets are safe with me …

and all my friends.

I don't repeat gossip.

So listen carefully.

Do

you

believe

in love

at first

sight?

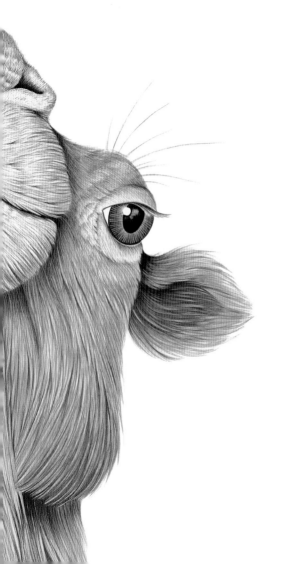

Or

should

I walk

past

again?

Anyone can be passionate.

But it takes real lovers to be silly.

Too much of a good thing

can be wonderful.

If you leave me ...

can I come too ?

The moment

you have children,

you forgive

your parents …

everything.

The

quickest

way for

a parent

to get a

child's

attention ...

is

to

sit

down

and

look

comfortable.

There are few things more satisfying

than seeing your children

have teenagers of their own.

You can't stay

young forever.

But you

can be

immature

for the

rest of your life.

I want it all -

and I want it delivered!

I didn't claw my way

to the top of the food chain

to eat roughage!

Never eat more

than you can lift.

It's been lovely.

But I have to s c r e a m now.

Artist's notes

Writing these notes brings with it the realization that this little book must finally be finished. Up until now the book has consistently refused to be finished, as it has been too tempting to keep adding new quotes and illustrations.

All the paintings are watercolor, built up in layers starting with the lightest tones first and finishing with the darkest shades. A tiny sable brush with a single hair at its tip allows me to get the detail I'm after. The single hair inevitably wears away by the end of each painting- sometimes annoyingly part way through. I always start with the eyes of the animal and if I manage to get the right expression in the eyes, then the painting generally turns out. If not, then I start over.

Researching the paintings can turn up a few surprises. There really is a blue-footed booby (page 9) who dances about from foot to foot so as not to be confused with any other sort of booby when impressing a potential mate.

And spare a thought for the little weaver bird on page 27 (*The trouble with work is…*). If he hasn't attracted a mate by the time the grass in the nest he has painstakingly built turns brown then he has to start over. Females are only interested in the nests that are fresh and green. So the pressure is on.

Furry Logic is a collection of the little challenges that life throws at us on a daily basis. If your little challenges are the same as some of the ones in this book, chances are you will have smiled, laughed even, in recognition. I hope so.

Best wishes,

Jane.

www.furrylogicbooks.com

Acknowledgements

Heartfelt thanks to the following very special people on whom Furry Logic depended upon in different ways for its start in the world: Mark Seabrook-Davison, Diana Robinson, Burton Silver, Mark Seabrook and Hugh Seabrook.

A great many other people all added their words of encouragement along the way and I would also like to thank Diana Cheney, Alison Davison, Kel Geddes, Greg Spode, Brett and Lisa Seabrook and Mabs Wiseman.

Thank you to the people at Image Centre, especially Andy Mackie, Troy Caltaux and Alex Trimbach; to PQ Publishing for seeing the possibilities in the early drafts and to Joy Willis at Phoenix Asia Pacific who expertly coordinated the printing process.

Grateful thanks to Ashleigh Brilliant for *I try to take one day at a time, but sometimes several days attack me at once.* www.ashleighbrilliant.com

Thank you also to John Cooney of Grapevine magazine, Auckland, New Zealand, for many of the quotations attributable to 'Anon'.

Other quotations appeared or are quoted in the following publications:

Be yourself. Nobody is better qualified. (Anon.) in 'More Pocket Positives', Five Mile Press, Melbourne, Australia; *If at first you do succeed, try not to look too astonished.* (Anon.) in 'World's Best Humour', Five Mile Press, Melbourne, Australia; *I never made Who's Who but I'm featured in What's That.* (Phyllis Diller), *Never go to bed mad- stay up and fight.* (Phyllis Diller) and *You can't stay young forever. But you can be immature for the rest of your life* (Maxine Wilkie) in 'Women's Lip', ed. Roz Warren, Sourcebook Inc., USA; If you don't agree with me, it means you haven't been listening. (Sam Markewich) in 'Comedy Comes Clean 2', Three Rivers Press, NY, USA; *If you leave me, can I come too?* (Cynthia Hemmel) in 'The Penguin Dictionary of Modern Humorous Quotations', ed. Fred Metcalf, Penguin Group, UK.

While every effort has been made to trace copyright holders of the quotations, the publisher would be very pleased to hear from any not acknowledged here to make amends in future printings.

www.crownpublishing.com

www.tenspeed.com

Ten Speed Press and the Ten Speed Press colophon are registered trademarks of
Random House, inc.
Library of Congress Cataloging-in-Publication Data on file with the publisher.

ISBN 978-1-58008-569-4
Printed in China

15 16 17 18 19—13 12 11 10 09

First Edition